Adam Hamilton

John

The Gospel of Light and Life

Youth Study Book
by Josh Tinley

Abingdon Press
Nashville

John
The Gospel of Light and Life

Youth Study Book
by Josh Tinley

This book is printed on elemental chlorine-free paper.

ISBN 978-1-501-80548-6

15 16 17 18 19 20 21 22 23 24—10 9 8 7 6 5 4 3 2 1

MANUFACTURED IN THE UNITED STATES OF AMERICA

CONTENTS

INTRODUCTION:
THE FOURTH GOSPEL

The first four books of the New Testament are called "Gospels." The word *gospel* literally means "good news," and each of these four books tells the good news about Jesus Christ through the story of his life, death, and resurrection. So why are there four of them? Wouldn't one account of Jesus' life be sufficient?

Perhaps. But each of the Gospel writers—Matthew, Mark, Luke, and John—includes stories and perspectives that are unique to his book. Some of our most popular stories about Jesus appear in only one Gospel: the wise men who visit baby Jesus show up only in Matthew; Luke is the only Gospel to include the parable of the prodigal son; and only John tells us about Jesus raising Lazarus from the dead.

Despite these differences, three of the Gospels are very similar. Matthew, Mark, and Luke include many of the same stories and sayings and present many of them in the same order. For this reason scholars often call them the "Synoptic" Gospels; *synoptic* is a Greek word meaning "seeing together." John, on the other hand, is radically different.

The Synoptic Gospels record Jesus' teachings, tell stories about his ministry, and show us how we can follow Jesus faithfully. John does something more. John explores the identity and meaning of Jesus. He explains how Jesus is God in human form; he illustrates what it means for Jesus to be the Word of God and the light of the world; and he shows us how we can have a personal relationship with God through Jesus.

As you study John, reflect on these questions:

- What is John saying about Jesus?
- How does Jesus give us life?
- How should I live in response to what Jesus has done?

Take a Tour Through John

This study focuses on six major parts or themes of John's Gospel:

- John's Prologue: John introduces Christ as the Word of God and the light of the world.
- Jesus' signs: John shows us seven miraculous signs that Jesus performs, showing us his divinity.
- Jesus' "I AM" statements: Jesus reveals his identity through several statements that begin with "I Am."
- Jesus' farewell address: John devotes multiple chapters to the talk Jesus gives his disciples on the night before his death.
- Jesus' arrest, trial, and death: John shows us that Jesus is completely in control of the events leading to his execution.
- Jesus' resurrection: Jesus defeats death, allowing us to enjoy the gift of eternal life.

As you examine each of these parts and themes, you will gain a greater understanding of what it means for Jesus to be God in human form, how Jesus won our salvation, and what Jesus' story means for us and how we live.

Depending on time and interest, you or your group might also consider reading John's Gospel in its entirety. One way to do this is to follow the plan below, reading the chapters in John that roughly correspond to each chapter in this book:

- Chapter 1: John 1
- Chapter 2: John 2–5
- Chapter 3: John 6–11
- Chapter 4: John 12–17
- Chapter 5: John 18–19
- Chapter 6: John 20–21

After reading each portion of John, reflect on or discuss the following:

- What was familiar to you about these chapters?
- What was new or surprising to you?
- What do these chapters tell us about who Jesus is?
- What do these chapters tell us about how we should live as followers of Jesus?

Using This Resource

This Youth Study Book is designed as a group study but also can be used for personal reading and devotion. Each session begins with a short chapter for individual reading. Those using this study can read these short chapters on their own or can set aside time for personal reading during their group meetings.

Sessions also include a variety of activities and discussion prompts for groups. Each session begins with an optional gathering activity. Then some activities are given that involve the large group. Finally the large group will split into smaller groups based on interests and talents, such as music, visual art, drama, science, and history. Depending on the time allotted, the smaller groups may want to present to the large group what they have learned or created.

Several activities invite participants to reflect on and discuss personal goals, feelings, and experiences with a partner or small group. It is essential that all group members treat their fellow participants with love and respect. Any personal information that becomes known during group discussion should be treated as confidential and received without judgment.

Enjoy this time you have to learn and reflect on John, the Gospel of light and life.

1

THE WORD MADE FLESH

In the beginning was the Word and the Word was with God and the Word was God. The Word was with God in the beginning. Everything came into being through the Word, and without the Word nothing came into being. (John 1:1-3)

The New Testament includes four Gospels: Matthew, Mark, Luke, and John. All four tell the story of Jesus' life, ministry, death, and resurrection. While some key events—Jesus' baptism, his feeding of the multitudes, his trial, and his crucifixion, among others—appear in all four books, each author emphasizes different aspects of Jesus' story.

We'd expect these writers to begin their stories with Jesus' birth, but only two of them do. Luke gives us the Christmas story that we read each December, with the shepherds and the host of angels. In Matthew we meet the wise men, who travel many miles to pay tribute to baby Jesus. Mark, on the other hand, skips all this and opens with Jesus as a full-grown man at his baptism.

John, like Mark, doesn't cover any of the material about the birth of Jesus. But one could make the case that John is the only Gospel that actually starts at the beginning of Jesus' story. Matthew and Luke tell us about Jesus' birth and give us lists of his ancestors, back to David and Bathsheba, Abraham and Sarah, even Adam and Eve. But John goes back even further to the start of all creation: "In the beginning was the Word and the Word was with God and the Word was God" (John 1:1).

Wordage

What do you think of when you hear the phrase *Word of God*? Often we associate God's Word with the Bible. But for John, the "Word" isn't a collection of books; it is Jesus Christ himself. Though Jesus spent thirty-some years living on earth as a human being, we know that he is also God and has existed for all time and will live for eternity. Matthew, Mark, and Luke focus mostly on Jesus' human life. John is different. He wants us to know that Jesus is God, and he gets his point across by telling us that Christ—the Word—was present and active when God created all things.

The Greek word for "Word" in these verses is *logos*, which is the root of the English words *logic* and *logical*. Stoicism, a school of ancient Greek philosophy, considered the *Logos* the mind and purpose of God at work throughout the entire universe. For that reason we often use *log* to refer to the study of something. You probably get your fill of *logos* every day when you study bio*log*y, socio*log*y, geo*log*y, psycho*log*y, and cosmeto*log*y.

The *logos* was a well-known concept in Jesus' day. But what John says in 1:14 would have rubbed a lot of people the wrong way: "The Word became flesh and made his home among us." Claiming that the Logos lived on earth as a human being was scandalous. John was telling his readers that Jesus was God's heart, mind, and will in human form.

We call this idea *Incarnation*. You may recognize the root *carn* from words like *carnivore* and *carnage*. It comes from Latin and means "flesh." While Christians for centuries have struggled to explain exactly how Jesus could be human and God at the same time, John tells us what is most important about the Incarnation: "No one has ever seen God. God the only Son, who is at the Father's side, has made God known" (John 1:18). In Jesus, God became one of us and gave us a picture of who God is, what God values, and how God relates to us.

God's Flashlight

John uses the language of light and darkness throughout his Gospel, starting with his fourth verse: "the Word was life, and the life was the light for all people." Light allows us to see; it carries information from one place to another; and it provides energy. When we "see the light," we have a moment of clarity or a realization of what is right or true. Darkness, of course, is the absence of light.

Metaphorically it refers to being lost, to times of despair and destruction, or to evil. Those with wicked tendencies are said to be on the "dark side" (a phrase popularized by the *Star Wars* movies).

Plenty of people in Jesus' day lived in darkness, as do plenty of people in our world today. Darkness can take the form of despair, grief, illness, violence, or spiritual longing, among other things. Light for the world cuts through that darkness, offering new life and new hope. If you've ever been caving or camping in a remote area, you appreciate having a source of light that can cut through the darkness. The illumination provided by a flashlight or lantern is often the difference between moving about safely or getting lost, injured, or panicked.

No matter how intense the darkness, Christ's light will always break through, guiding us and giving us hope. We never have to worry about dead batteries!

Live Eternally Now

John's opening verses also tell us that the Word offers us life. Many Christians and non-Christians alike are familiar with John's most famous verse, from 3:16: "God so loved the world that he gave his only Son, so that everyone who believes in him won't perish but will have eternal life." Something that is eternal goes on forever. We usually think of eternal life beginning after our deaths. But we don't have to wait. When we trust and enter into a relationship with Christ, we defeat death and start living eternally now.

While we are still in this world, our eternal lives will not spare us from the struggles and weaknesses that come with being human. But we can face these challenges with the confidence that they will not have the last word. We can live with the knowledge that Christ, the *Logos*, is in control; and we can reflect the light of Christ to those who are living in darkness.

A note on "John": The Gospel of John never identifies its author by name. It frequently refers to a disciple "whom Jesus loved." In the book's final verses, this unknown disciple says that he is the book's writer. In the other Gospels, John, along with James and Peter, is one of Jesus' closest disciples. But the disciple John isn't mentioned in the Gospel of John, leading many early Christians to assume that John must be the "disciple whom Jesus loved" and the author of the book.

In this study, we'll refer to the author of the book as "John," even though we don't know with certainty that "John" was actually his name.

Session 1 Activities

Gathering Activity (Optional)

Get Logical

John's Gospel refers to Jesus as the Word. The Greek translation of *Word* in these verses is *Logos*. *Logos* is the root of the words *logic* and *logical*, and many ancient Greek thinkers used *Logos* to refer to the wisdom and purpose of God. In honor of Christ, the *Logos*, try the logic puzzle shown on the next page, using the chart and clues that are given.

This puzzle will probably take more time than allotted for a gathering time. It can worked on as a gathering activity for each session. Answers can be found at the end of the book.

Large Group Activities

In the Beginning Was the Word

As a group, read through John 1:1-18, the Prologue to John's Gospel. Everyone should have some time to read through the verses silently. Then read the scripture aloud. Each person can read aloud one verse. Rotate around the room until the entire Prologue has been read. Then ask:

- Who, or what, is the "Word" in this Scripture?
- What do these verses tell us about God and how God works?
- What questions do you have after reading this Scripture?

List any questions that members of your group have on a markerboard or large sheet of paper. You will refer back to these later.

Get Logical

James, John, Martha, Mary, and Peter are headed to Jerusalem to celebrate the Passover. Each person is coming from a different city—Alexandria, Antioch, Corinth, Ephesus, and Rome. Each person also is bringing a different food item to the festival—bread, figs, fish, olive oil, and wine. Using the clues below, determine who is coming from what city and which food item he or she is bringing.

1. The man from Corinth brought a liquid.
2. The woman from Rome also brought a liquid.
3. The man who brought the bread and the man who brought the fish both came from a cities whose names start with the letter "A."
4. Martha brought a food whose name starts with the letter "F."
5. Peter also brought a food whose name starts with the letter "F."
6. A woman brought the olive oil.
7. James did not bring the bread, and neither did the man from Antioch.

The best way to solve a logic problem is to use a chart like the one below. Start by using a process of elimination. For example, the first clue, "The man from Corinth brought a liquid," doesn't tell you who came from Corinth. It does however say something about who didn't come from Corinth. So in the "Corinth" column put and x in the box corresponding to any people you know for sure aren't from that city. When you find a match, mark it with a circle, smiley face, or check mark.

	Alexandria	Antioch	Corinth	Ephesus	Rome	Bread	Figs	Fish	Olive Oil	Wine
James										
John										
Martha										
Mary										
Peter										
Bread										
Figs										
Fish										
Olive Oil										
Wine										

Who Is This "John" Guy?

John was a very common name in the first-century Jewish world, and scholars have different theories about which John wrote the New Testament books attributed to John (the Gospel of John, the three Letters of John, and the Revelation to John). The Gospel of John never actually names its author, so it's possible that the writer wasn't even named John. At any rate, there is one major biblical figure named John who most definitely didn't write any of these books: John the Baptist.

In the Prologue, when verse 6 says, "A man named John was sent from God," the author is not referring to himself but to John the Baptist. To better understand who John the Baptist is and why he is important, read the following scriptures. Depending on group size and time, the entire group can read all the scriptures, or you can divide into teams and assign one scripture to each. After reading these verses, brainstorm a list of things you know about John the Baptist.

- Matthew 3:1-15
- Luke 3:7-20
- John 1:6-18
- John 1:19-34

Once you have a pretty good list, discuss:

- Why do you think the Gospel writers emphasize John the Baptist so much toward the beginning of their stories?
- How is John the Baptist similar to Jesus? In what ways is he different?

Start Living Forever

In taking on human form and living among us, Christ invited us to new, eternal life. Often we think of eternal life as something that begins after we die. But we don't have to wait. We can start living forever right now.

Read through Live Eternally Now in the opening of this session. Then divide a markerboard or large sheet of paper into two columns. Label one column "Right Now" and another "Later On." Brainstorm things that people living eternal life with Christ can look forward to. Put each item in the appropriate column. For example, "Working with God to heal those who are hurting" could go in the "Right Now" column. "An end to all suffering" could go in the "Later On" column. It's possible that some items will fit into both columns.

After you have lots of items in both columns, pair off. Each person should think of one way he or she can enjoy eternal life this week. These ways of enjoying eternal life should be specific and achievable. Partners should hold each other accountable—by text messages, face-to-face conversations, or social media—for what they choose to do.

Small Group Activities

Divide into teams based on interest. There are activities for music, visual art, drama and comedy, and science.

Word and Music (music)

The first eighteen verses of John's Gospel may come from an early Christian hymn. Recover the musical side of John's opening verses by taking part or all of John 1:1-18 and setting them to music. Your group can turn these verses into a song in your favorite musical genre, or you can set them to the music of an existing song. Put together an a capella version of this scripture or use a guitar, keyboard, or drum machine app on a smartphone or other device to provide accompaniment. Use a smartphone camera or audio recorder to record your song or prepare to perform it for the rest of your group.

Put Flesh On It (visual art)

John 1:14 says, "The Word became flesh and made his home among us." In other words, the Word—God's heart, mind, and will—became a human being, Jesus Christ.

Brainstorm a list of abstract ideas, such as "kindness" or "persistence" or "comfort." After there is a good list, participants can be divided into pairs or teams of three and each pair or team can select one item from the list. (Each team should be working with a different abstract idea.) Pairs and teams will put flesh on" their ideas by drawing and/or describing in writing a person who embodies this concept.

Who's the Word? (drama, comedy)

Watch the classic Abbott and Costello comedy sketch "Who's on First" on YouTube or another video service. Work with your pair or team to create a comedy sketch around the opening verses of the Gospel of John. ("In the beginning was the Word." "What word?" "The Word was God?" "So 'God' is the Word?")

You may write a script for your sketch, or you may improvise. Just make sure you have some record of your work, whether as a written script, a phone video, or a live performance for the rest of the group. When you're finished, or as you work, consider the following questions:

- What is hard to understand about the Prologue to John's Gospel?
- What might be especially confusing for someone who has not spent time in the church and is not familiar with Scripture?
- How would you explain these verses about "the Word" in a way that is easy to understand?

Create a Prism (science)

Supplies: cup of water, flashlight, large sheet of white paper or cloth

You've probably learned in science class that light contains all the colors of the spectrum. Ordinarily light appears white. but there are ways to disperse light and separate it so that it appears like a rainbow. A prism is one device for dispersing light. Prisms vary in shape, style, and substance, but they consist of transparent materials such as water and glass.

When light moves from one medium to another—such as from air to glass to water—it changes speed, causing it to bend. The degree to which the light bends depends on its wavelength; each wavelength appears as a different color. So when light passes through a prism, every color of light bends at a unique angle, dividing the light into many colors.

Create and experiment with a prism of your own:

- Fill a glass with water so it is mostly full.
- Place the glass on a table (preferably one low to the ground, such as a coffee table) so that it hangs over the edge. Watch it carefully to make sure that it doesn't fall.

- Set a large sheet of white paper or cloth on the floor beneath the cup. (If you have a white tile floor, don't worry about this step.)
- Hold a flashlight above the glass and shine it downward, through the water and onto the floor.
- Adjust the angle of the flashlight as needed until you see the light separate into colors.

Then discuss:

- When the light hits the water and glass, it bends and separates. What happens when the light of Christ hits the earth?
- White light is made up of all the colors of the rainbow. What is the light of Christ made up of? (Examples might include: hope, justice, and so forth.)

• • •

Teams should have plenty of time to work, then each team or pair can present its work to the large group. Then discuss:

- Whom have you known who seemed to embody a certain characteristic or idea? (Stick to positive examples only.)
- Read John 1:1-5. What do these verses say about "the Word"?
- What does it mean for Jesus to be the Word in human form? What does this tell you about Jesus?
- What qualities should we embody as Jesus' followers? How can we take on these qualities?

Closing

Revisit the questions you wrote down for the large group activity called "In the Beginning Was the Word." See which questions you can answer now that you've read and studied John 1:1-18. (Keep track of questions you cannot answer and review these in future sessions.) Then close in prayer.

God of Word and light, thank you for putting on flesh and living among us. Thank you for cutting through the darkness and showing us the path of eternal light. Guide us as we strive to embody the love and grace you've shown us; and give us the strength and courage to claim your gift of eternal life here and now. Amen.

17

2

THE MIRACULOUS SIGNS OF JESUS

On the third day there was a wedding in Cana of Galilee. Jesus'
mother was there, and Jesus and his disciples were also invited to
the celebration. When the wine ran out, Jesus' mother said to him,
"They don't have any wine." Jesus replied, "Woman, what does
that have to do with me? My time hasn't come yet." His mother
told the servants, "Do whatever he tells you." (John 2:1-5)

As Jesus walked along, he saw a man who was blind from birth.
Jesus' disciples asked, "Rabbi, who sinned so that he was born
blind, this man or his parents?" Jesus answered, "Neither he nor
his parents. This happened so that God's mighty works might be
displayed in him. (John 9:1-3)

You've probably learned from your English teachers (and possibly from teachers
of other subjects as well) the value of supporting your claims and arguments with
evidence. Even if your teacher agrees with your views on health care, for example,
you won't get a good grade on your health care essay if you don't back up your
viewpoint with examples and research.

The author of the Gospel of John would make any English teacher happy (even
though he wrote his book in Greek). He has an argument: Jesus is the Christ. And
he has evidence to back up his claim: Jesus performed several remarkable feats
that prove who he is. We usually refer to these feats as miracles. John calls them
miraculous signs.

Boom! Wine!

Jesus' first miraculous sign in John's Gospel happens at a wedding in a town called Cana. Weddings today usually are followed by a meal or reception. The same was true of first-century Jewish weddings, with one major difference: ancient Jewish wedding feasts are believed to have lasted seven days. That's quite a catering gig.

At some point during this weeklong celebration, the wine ran out. After his mother informed him there was no more wine, Jesus had the servants fill some jars with water. When the waiter drew water from one of the jars, it had become wine. According to John, turning water to wine was Jesus' first miraculous sign. After witnessing this miracle, the disciples believed he was the Messiah.

Changing water to wine didn't confirm that Jesus was the Messiah just because it was miraculous; it was also a symbolic act. The jars that Jesus used were "jars used for the Jewish cleansing ritual" (John 2:6). People who had become ritually unclean would perform rituals that would restore them to the community and make them whole.

John also tells us that, when the servants at the wedding filled the jars, they filled them to the brim, almost overflowing. After the water became wine, the headwaiter tasted it and found that it was even better than the "good wine" from earlier in the festivities.

Each aspect of this story symbolizes what Jesus does for us:

- The jars used for cleansing represent how Jesus cleanses and restores us. He died to atone for our sins and offers us forgiveness, making us new and whole.
- The way the servants filled the jars to the brim represents how Jesus fills us with love and grace and the power of the Holy Spirit.
- The quality of the new wine represents how Jesus perfects us and makes us new. The significance of this first miraculous sign was not lost on Jesus' disciples. John 2:11 says, "[Jesus] revealed his glory, and his disciples believed in him."

Seeing the Light

John tells us of seven miraculous signs that Jesus performed. Four of these seven involved miraculous healings. The Bible shows us that God can and does heal all manner of human ailments and injuries. While these healings are evidence of God's love and power, they also raise some uncomfortable questions: Why are some people healed but not others? If God has power over disease, why do people become ill in the first place?

Jesus' disciples seem to have wrestled with some of these questions and come to a conclusion. When they approached a man born blind in John 9, they asked Jesus, "[Who] sinned so that he was born blind, this man or his parents?" (v. 2). They assumed that the man's blindness was a punishment—that God wouldn't allow a good person to have such a severe impairment.

But Jesus wasn't interested in placing the blame on anyone. Jesus had a different take on the situation. He told his disciples that neither the man nor his parents sinned. The man's blindness "happened so that God's mighty works might be displayed in him" (v. 3). Jesus then "spit on the ground, made mud with the saliva, and smeared the mud on the man's eyes" (v. 6).

It may sound gross, but it worked. Jesus told the man to wash in a pool outside the city. The man did so and was able to see. Some religious leaders in the area took issue with this healing. They weren't convinced that the man had actually been blind (vv. 8-9). They didn't understand how someone they considered a sinner—Jesus—could muster the power to give a blind man sight (vv. 17, 24-34). And they were upset that Jesus had healed the man on the sabbath, a day set aside for rest according to the Ten Commandments. For John, these religious leaders missed the mark. They were so caught up in their understanding of the law and how things should work that they failed to appreciate the miracle. The blind man, by contrast, was too excited to let the religious leaders get him down. He was convinced that Jesus came from God and, for that reason, was able to give him sight.

Just as the miraculous sign in Cana was about more than wine, this miraculous sign was about more than just giving a blind man sight. In the closing verses of John 9, Jesus explained that he hadn't come just to heal those who are physically blind; he was more concerned with those who are spiritually blind.

When we enter into a relationship with Christ, we see everything in a new way. Our eyes are opened to all that God is doing around us.

See the Sign, Be the Sign

Most of us probably haven't experienced something as incredible as water transforming to wine or a blind person suddenly receiving sight. But we nonetheless may have seen signs of God's love, presence, and work. God may be revealed to us in the form of encouragement from a teacher or coach, of an opportunity to serve by volunteering at an assisted-living facility or tutoring grade school children, or of an emotional moment during worship. These signs bring us hope, joy, and relief in the moment but also point toward greater truths about God: God loves us, guides us, provides for us, and has high expectations for us. These signs are evidence that we can cite in support of our faith and trust in God.

Sometimes we are the signs. God might work through you to lift the spirits of a friend or peer. God might use your gifts and talents to inspire others in your congregation or community. God may take a small act of kindness and turn it into something greater than you could ever imagine. We know what God has done in the person of Christ, and we know that God can do equally amazing things through each of us. We can be the evidence that others point to in support of their faith and trust in God.

As Jesus' followers, we should embrace God's gift of sight—spiritual sight. We must keep our eyes open so we will witness and learn from God's signs and wonders. And we must keep our hearts open so that God can do signs and wonders through us.

Session 2 Activities

Gathering Activity (Optional)

Get Logical

If you have not yet had time to finish it, continue working on the logic puzzle from Session 1. If you finish, check your answers with others in the group before looking at the answers at the end of the book. Remember that the inspiration for this activity comes from the opening chapter of John, which refers to Christ using the Greek word *Logos*, which is the root of the words *logic* and *logical*.

Large Group Activities

I Need a Sign

Before getting into the Gospel of John, go back to the Old Testament and read aloud Judges 6:11-24. Then discuss:

- Who is the main character in this scripture?
- What does God ask of this person?
- How does this person respond?
- Was this person right to respond this way? Why or why not?

Take a moment to reflect on times you've wanted a sign from God or times when you've seen evidence of God's presence. Discuss:

- When have you wanted a sign from God?
- What signs have you seen of God's presence in your life?
- Are signs from God important for faith? Why or why not?

See the Signs

The Gospel of John refers to Jesus' works as miraculous signs. There are seven such miraculous signs in John. Participants should be divided into pairs or teams of three, and each pair or team assigned one or more of the following scriptures. (All seven scriptures should be assigned.)

- John 2:1-11
- John 4:46-54
- John 5:1-18
- John 6:5-14
- John 6:16-24
- John 9:1-7
- John 11:1-45

Each team should read its assigned scripture and be prepared to tell the rest of the group:

- What miraculous sign does Jesus perform in these verses?
- What does this miraculous sign tell us about Jesus?
- Is there anything symbolic about this miraculous sign? Does the miracle represent something or tell us some greater truth about Jesus?

Small Group Activities

Teams can be divided based on interest. There are activities for music, visual art, drama and comedy, and science.

Reception Playlist (music)

Jesus' first miraculous sign in John's Gospel is changing water to wine at a wedding feast in the town of Cana. This feat was a sign not only because it defied the laws of nature but also because the jars Jesus used and the words he said were symbolic.

Add another layer of symbolism to the wedding at Cana story by taking a job as the DJ at the wedding feast described in John. Come up with a playlist consisting of songs that offer some hints about who Jesus is and what he came to do. Since you will be traveling back in time to take this job, you can bring with you songs from the twentieth and twenty-first centuries. Stick with popular songs (rock, hip hop, R&B, country, and so forth) from recent decades (nothing earlier than the 1960s). You may include praise and worship songs, but avoid tracks that come out and say, "Jesus is Lord." Find music that is subtle, such as songs that use common metaphors for Jesus (light, word, bread).

Be prepared to name the songs on your playlist and explain their significance.

Transform It and Make It Whole (visual art)

Supplies: paper (either individual sheets or one large sheet), black ink pens or markers, colored markers or pencils

You can do this activity individually or as a team.

Start by taking a sheet of paper (a standard 8 1/2-by-11 sheet of paper for individuals, a sheet of poster paper for a team) and scribble on it in a black ink pen or marker. Don't scribble too densely; you want to leave spaces in between the scribble lines.

Your paper at this point should be a mess of scribbles. You will take this mess and turn it into art by coloring the spaces between the scribbles with markers or colored pencils. You can fill in the spaces to make an abstract design or look for pictures and patterns to create something more concrete. While you're working, discuss:

- Think about some of Jesus' signs, especially turning water into wine and giving the blind man sight. How did Jesus take something messy or broken and turn it into something beautiful?
- How has God given you gifts and opportunities to bring beauty to an ugly situation?
- What is something small that you could do in the next two weeks that would bring beauty to brokenness? (This could involve mending a relationship with someone or helping someone in your community in need of assistance.)
- Do you know someone who has shown signs of God's love and healing power? What can you learn from this person's example?

Be prepared to show your artwork and summarize your discussion.

Pass the Blame (drama)

Work together to create a skit about a group of people who end up in an unfortunate situation and want to find someone to blame. In your skit, these people should spend so much time worrying about who is at fault that they don't get around to doing anything to make their situation better. Write a script for your skit, or prepare to perform it for the rest of the group.

After you've finished your skit, discuss:

- How are the people in your skit similar to the disciples in John 9?
- Based on your skit and John 9, what happens when we focus so much energy on finding someone to blame? How could that energy be put to better use?

Be prepared to summarize your discussion for the others.

Mir-egg-ulous (science)

Supplies: hard-boiled egg, glass bottle, lighter or match, strip of paper; a little bit of oil is optional

For this activity you will need a hard-boiled egg, a glass bottle whose mouth is slightly smaller than the diameter of the egg (such as a 16-ounce bottle of juice or a fruit drink), a lighter or match, and a strip of paper.

Peel the shell from the egg and set it atop the bottle to make sure that it is larger than the bottle and won't slide through the opening.

Then remove the egg from the top of the bottle. Use the match or lighter to light the strip of paper. Drop the burning strip of paper into bottle. While the paper is still burning, place the egg on the opening of the bottle. After a few seconds, the bottle should suck the egg through the opening. It's a miracle!

(You might place some oil on around the mouth of the bottle to help the egg go through smoothly, without breaking.)

Why does this work? The fire from the burning strip of paper causes the air to expand. When you place the egg on top of the bottle and the fire goes out, the air starts to cool and contract. When the air contracts, the pressure on the inside of the bottle becomes less than the pressure on the outside. The greater outside air pressure pushes the egg through the mouth of the bottle.

Most of the miracles in John have some greater significance. Changing water in stone jars into wine may represent how God, through Christ, transforms our hearts of stone. The blind man receiving sight is similar to each person "seeing the light" when he or she accepts a relationship with Christ. With this in mind, come up with a meaning or metaphor for your egg-in-the-bottle metaphor. What might the egg represent? What might the bottle represent? Why might the large egg falling through the smaller mouth of the bottle be significant? Could the fire have some meaning?

Be prepared to explain your metaphor to the group.

• • •

The teams should have plenty of time to complete their activities. Then each group can present what it did, created, and/or discussed. Following the presentations, discuss:

- What did you learn from these presentations about how God speaks to us through signs and wonders?
- What else did you learn from these presentations about Christ, our relationship with Christ, and how we live as Christ's followers?

Closing

To close, review what you've learned and discussed by examining the following three questions. Everyone should have some time to reflect, then go around the room and each person should answer one or more of the questions.

- What have you learned from this session about how John sees Jesus and particularly how John sees Jesus' miracles?
- As a result of our time together, do you see any events in your life as signs of God's love and presence?
- In what ways might you be a sign of God's love, grace, and healing? What might others learn from your example and experiences?

Then close in prayer.

God of signs and wonders, thank you for all the amazing ways you've entered our world. As we leave here, open our eyes to see all the ways you are at work among us and all the reminders of your love for us. Use us, that our lives and works might be signs for those who are seeking you. In the name of the One who transforms and heals we pray. Amen.

3

THE "I AM" SAYINGS OF JESUS

*But Moses said to God, "If I now come to the Israelites and say
to them, 'The God of your ancestors has sent me to you,' they are
going to ask me, 'What's this God's name?' What am I supposed to
say to them?" God said to Moses, "I Am Who I Am. So say to the
Israelites, 'I Am has sent me to you.'" (Exodus 3:13-14)*

*"Your father Abraham was overjoyed that he would see my day.
He saw it and was happy." "You aren't even 50 years old!" the
Jewish opposition replied. "How can you say that you have seen
Abraham?" "I assure you," Jesus replied, "before Abraham was,
I Am." (John 8:56-58)*

What is God's name? Most of the names we use for God aren't really names
but titles, like *Lord* or *Father*. As Christians we know that God became human
and took the name *Jesus*. We might also talk about God using names given to the
Holy Spirit, such as *Comforter* or *Advocate*.

Way back in the Old Testament, when God gave Moses the job of delivering
the Israelites from slavery in Egypt, Moses decided to ask for God's name. Moses
had fled from Egypt years earlier and was living in another land when God spoke
to him from a burning bush and told him to take on the most powerful nation
in that part of the world. Moses didn't want this job. However, if he was going to
do it, he felt he should at least know the name of this "God" who had hired him.

God obliged. Kind of. "I Am Who I Am," God told Moses. "So say to the Israelites, 'I Am has sent me to you' " (Exodus 3:14). It was a strange answer, but it stuck. The actual name, in Hebrew, is always written without vowels and can be translated either "I Am Who I Am," "I Will Be Who I Will Be," or just "I Am." In English it comes out as "YHWH," usually pronounced *Yahweh*. The name was considered so sacred by the Israelites and their Jewish descendants that they substituted another name, *Adonai*.

In John 8, Jesus was talking to some religious leaders about Abraham in a way that suggested Jesus had spoken to Abraham personally. The problem was, Abraham died more than a thousand years before Jesus was born. This wasn't an issue for Jesus, who told these religious leaders, "Before Abraham was, I Am" (John 8:58). The religious leaders were furious, not because Jesus was claiming to be some sort of time traveler or because his grammar didn't seem quite right, but because he called himself, "I Am." Jesus was claiming to be God.

I Am ... Well, Lots of Things

We usually think of the religious leaders in John 8 as the bad guys, but how would you respond to someone who claimed to be God? Would you think that person was crazy? delusional? dangerously arrogant?

Here's a fun vocabulary word that probably won't help you on your ACT tests: *Christology*. *Christology* describes how one understands Christ. Someone with a "low Christology" thinks of Jesus mainly as a great human teacher and prophet. Someone with a "high Christology" focuses more on Jesus as divine—as God. The Gospel of John has a higher Christology than any other Gospel. We see this in the Prologue (1:1-18), which we discussed in Session 1; we see this in the miraculous signs that Jesus performed; and we see it in the way that Jesus spoke about himself.

Eight times in John, Jesus referred to himself using "I am." Each time he revealed something about his identity and his relationship with us. By calling himself the "bread of life," he told us that he sustains us, much as food sustains our bodies. By calling himself the "light of the world," he told us that he cuts through the darkness and shows us the way forward. By calling himself the "resurrection and the life," he told us that he offers us a life that will not succumb to death.

Some who heard these words from Jesus were upset; some even responded with violence. But Jesus was able to back up his words. He showed that he had God's power to create and heal; he gave us an example of how to live life entirely according to God's will; he sacrificed himself to save us; and he defeated death to offer us the gifts of resurrection and eternal life.

Bread? Light?

Often Jesus' "I AM" statements corresponded to his signs (the ones we looked at in Chapter 2), his teachings, or a particular situation. For instance, before raising his friend Lazarus from the dead, Jesus told Lazarus's sister Martha, "I am the resurrection and the life" (John 11:25). Before his death and resurrection, Jesus told his disciples that he was going to his Father and that he would prepare a place for them. When they asked how to get to the place he was going, Jesus answered, "I am the way, the truth, and the life" (John 14:6).

Another of Jesus' "I AM" statements followed Jesus' feeding thousands of people with only a few fishes and loaves of bread. John tells us that, following this miracle, Jesus and his disciples crossed the Sea of Galilee, the disciples by boat and Jesus by foot. The crowd he had fed soon found him on the other side of the lake. Jesus had fed all of them using limited resources, and they wanted to see more. Jesus told them, "Don't work for the food that doesn't last but for the food that endures for eternal life" (John 6:27). His audience didn't quite understand what Jesus was talking about, so he went on to say, "I am the bread of life. Whoever comes to me will never go hungry, and whoever believes in me will never be thirsty" (John 6:35).

The people in the crowd took Jesus' words about bread literally. They had seen him miraculously provide bread for thousands of hungry people, and it brought to mind the history of their people. When the ancient Israelites were wandering through the desert after escaping slavery in Egypt, God provided them with water and food, including a strange bread from heaven called manna (Exodus 16). Though Jesus said that he, like the manna, had come from heaven, he wasn't announcing his intentions to start a catering business. Food, such as bread, is necessary for life, but its effects are temporary. Bread will only sustain us for so long before we feel hungry again. Jesus sustains us forever, not by providing nutrients, but by bringing us into a relationship with God that lasts an eternity.

One of Jesus' best-known sayings—"I am the light of the world. Whoever follows me won't walk in darkness but will have the light of life" (John 8:12)— is easier to understand if we know the setting. Jesus made this statement in the Temple during the Festival of Sukkot, also known as the Festival of Booths. The "booths" refer to the tents that the ancient Israelites set up while they were traveling through the desert on their way to the Promised Land. Just as God had provided food to the people of Israel during this difficult time, God also provided light, going before them as a column of fire or lightning so they could travel at night and know the way. In remembrance of this column of light, the Jews in Jerusalem lit lamps on four seventy-five-foot-tall lamp stands that illuminated the entire city.

Much as Jesus wasn't talking about wheat and yeast when he called himself bread, he wasn't talking about photons when he called himself light. "Walking in darkness" did not refer to traveling at night but being lost in sin and despair. Jesus, the light, offers us hope and forgiveness and comfort to lead us out of the darkness.

Jesus frequently called himself "I Am" both because he is God and because he is so many things to us. He is the shepherd who protects us, the bread that sustains us, the light that guides us, and the way that leads us to eternal life with God. By recording all these statements, John helps us better understand who Jesus is and what it means for us to have a relationship with him.

Session 3 Activities

Gathering Activity (Optional)

Get Logical

If you have not yet had time to finish it, continue working on the logic puzzle from Session 1. If you finish, check your answers with others in the group before looking at the answers at the end of the book. Remember that the inspiration for this activity comes from the opening chapter of John, which refers to Christ using the Greek word *Logos*, which is the root of the words *logic* and *logical*.

Large Group Activities

Who Am I?

Jesus in the Gospel of John refers to himself several times using the words *I Am*. That may not seem remarkable, but *I Am* is the name for God in the Old Testament. When he said, "I Am," Jesus was identifying himself as God.

Participants can be divided into pairs or groups of three. Each pair or team can take one or more of the following scriptures. All seven scriptures need to be assigned.

- John 6:26-40
- John 8:12-18
- John 10:1-10
- John 10:11-21
- John 11:17-44
- John 14:1-7
- John 15:1-8

Each team should read its assigned scripture and be prepared to tell the rest of the group:

- What is the "I AM" statement in these verses?
- What is the context? Where or when or in what situation does Jesus make this statement?
- What does this "I AM" statement say about who Jesus is?
- What does this "I AM" statement say about our relationship with Jesus?

Walking in Darkness

Read John 8:12-30. Discuss:

- What was Jesus saying about himself in this Scripture?
- What is unclear or confusing about what he was saying?

The Pharisees challenging Jesus were so worried about Jesus' claims that they missed what he said about being the "light of the world." Jesus taught, "Whoever follows me won't walk in darkness but will have the light of life" (John 8:12).

Divide a markerboard or large sheet of paper into two columns. Label one "Darkness" and the other "Light." Brainstorm ways in which people might be "walking in darkness" and list these in the darkness column. For instance, someone might suffer from grief or guilt or addiction. Then for each item in the darkness column, identify one way the light of Christ might overcome this darkness, and list it in the light column. For instance, Christ might respond to our darkness with comfort or forgiveness or the strength to overcome.

After you've filled in your two columns, discuss some ways that people in darkness experience the light of Christ. Specifically, talk about how God works through us to bring light to those in darkness.

Small Group Activities

Team can be divided based on interest. There are activities for music, drama, and cooking.

I Am, for the Children (music)

Use Jesus' "I AM" statements from the Gospel of John to create a children's song. Since the song is for children, it should follow a simple, repetitive pattern. One line should be an "I AM" statement; the next should say something about the "I AM" statement. For example,

Jesus says, "I am the resurrection and the life; I'll save you from death and I'll save you from strife."

You should have a total of eight pairs of lines, using the following statements:

- Before Abraham was, I Am.
- I am the bread of life.
- I am the light of the world.
- I am the gate of the sheep.
- I am the good shepherd.
- I am the resurrection and the life.
- I am the way, the truth, and the life.

Set your lines to a melody. You may also add a simple chorus to break things up. Be prepared to perform your song for the rest of the group. If possible, arrange to teach your song to a children's Sunday school class or Bible study group in your congregation.

What? No You Aren't! (drama)

Read John 8:52-59. In verse 58 Jesus says, "Before Abraham was, I Am." "I Am" is God's name, as revealed to Moses in the Old Testament. By saying, "Before Abraham was, I Am," Jesus was saying, "I am God." This was obviously a controversial statement and one that would have upset or confused many of those who heard him say it. Verse 59 says that some of the people in the temple were so angry that they threw stones at him.

Imagine what else might have been said between Jesus and the people in the temple after Jesus declared, "I Am." (For instance: "What did you just say? Did you call yourself, 'I Am'? Do you understand what that means?") One member of the team can play the role of Jesus; others can portray people at the temple.

Write a script for your scene and/or be prepared to act it out for the rest of the group. After you present your scene, ask the group:

- What does it mean to you that Jesus is God in human form? Why might this be difficult for people to understand or accept?
- How might you help people better understand who Jesus is and how Jesus relates to us?

"Bread of Life (cooking)

In John 6:35, Jesus says, "I am the bread of life. Whoever comes to me will never go hungry." Bread is a very basic food that will sustain our bodies. It is a staple of many diets in the twenty-first-century United States, and it was even more important in first-century Galilee and Judea, where Jesus lived and traveled. If you have the resources available at your church, make one type of bread that would have been familiar to Jesus and his disciples. God instructed the ancient Israelites to eat only unleavened bread—bread without leavening agents such as yeast—during the Passover festival. Jewish people to this day observe this custom. During his final meal with his disciples, Jesus would have broken and eaten unleavened bread. This type of bread is easy to make:

Ingredients:
- Two cups of whole wheat flour
- 1/2 cup of white flour
- 1 cup of water
- 1/8 cup of honey
- 1 teaspoon salt
- 1/8 cup oil

Mix the ingredients together to form a dough. Roll out the dough in a thin sheet and place onto a greased cookie sheet. Prick the dough with a fork, making rows about one-half inch apart. Cut the dough into squares approximately four inches in length and width, and separate them. Bake the dough for about 15 minutes at 400 degrees.

While you are working, discuss:

- Why do you think Jesus referred to himself as bread instead of some other food?
- In what ways does Jesus feed you and sustain you?

Be prepared to share your unleavened bread with the rest of the group. If you have a large group, you may need to double the recipe.

• • •

Give teams plenty of time to complete their activities. Then have each group present what it created or discussed. Following the presentations, discuss:

- What did you learn from these presentations about the ways Jesus identified himself?
- What else did you learn from these presentations about Christ, our relationship with Christ, and how we live as Christ's followers?

Closing

To close, each participant should select one of Jesus' seven "I AM" statements and come up with a statement in this form: "Because Jesus is…, I am…." For instance, "Because Jesus is the way, I am devoted to following him" or "Because Jesus is the bread of life, I have the energy to persevere." Everyone should have plenty of time to come up with an idea, then each person can say aloud his or her statement. Everyone's statement can be recorded on a markerboard or large sheet of paper. Then close in prayer.

Great I Am, thank you for this time we've had together, and thank you for John's Gospel and all the ways it helps us better understand who you are. As you light our path and show us your way, may we light the way for others. As you feed us and sustain us, may we be the bread of life for those who need it most. As you lived among us as God in human form, may we give others a glimpse of who God is and how God is at work in the world. Amen.

4

THE FAREWELL DISCOURSE

*"My Father is glorified when you produce much fruit and in
this way prove that you are my disciples. As the Father loved
me, I too have loved you. Remain in my love. If you keep my
commandments, you will remain in my love, just as I kept my
Father's commandments and remain in his love."*

(John 15:8-10)

As you get closer to graduation and adulthood, your life will be the source
of stress for numerous adults in your life. Regardless of how well behaved you
are, how responsible you are, or how successful you've been in school and other
activities, your parents, teachers, coaches, and youth ministers are going to worry.
They won't necessarily worry because they think you won't be able to handle the
pressures that will come your way. Rather, they'll worry that they haven't done
everything possible to prepare you.

On the night before his death, Jesus was in a situation similar to what your
parents and teachers will be in as you get ready to leave their care. He had one final
evening with his disciples—one last chance to prepare them for what would be
next. And much as none of us can really appreciate the challenges that come with
leaving high school and moving out until we actually do it, Jesus' disciples couldn't
really appreciate or understand what was in store for them.

All four of the Gospel writers give an account of Jesus' last night with his
disciples, but John goes into much greater detail. Luke devotes 25 verses to this
occasion (40 if you go through Jesus' prayer in the garden and arrest), more than
either Matthew or Mark. John, by comparison, uses 155 verses. Jesus' story in John

spans three years, but five of John's twenty-one chapters focus on this one evening. Jesus' preparation to leave his disciples is of great importance to John.

Dirty Feet

Jesus began this time with his disciples on the night before his death by washing their feet. In first-century Galilee and Judea where Jesus lived, most people traveled by foot, wearing either sandals or no shoes at all. Feet tended to get pretty nasty, and washing feet wasn't the sort of job anyone wanted to do. In fact, it was a job assigned to household servants. As a sign of hospitality and as a courtesy to road-weary travelers, servants would wash the feet of houseguests.

So when Jesus washed his disciples' dirty feet, he was taking the role of a servant. This caught the disciples off guard. If anyone should have been washing anyone's feet, they should have been washing his. Peter even protested, saying, "No! You will never wash my feet!" But Jesus insisted. "Unless I wash you," he told them, "you won't have a place with me" (John 13:8).

Jesus did this, not because he was overly concerned with his followers' hygiene but because he was setting an example. "If I, your Lord and teacher, have washed your feet," Jesus said, "you too must wash each other's feet. I have given you an example: just as I have done, you also must do" (John 13:14-15). While many Christians today take Jesus' words literally, and follow his example by doing foot-washing rituals each year during Holy Week, Jesus' teaching here isn't limited to getting the dirt off one another's soles and the grime out from between one another's toes. We are faithful to Jesus' teaching here when we humble ourselves and take the role of servants, whether by washing feet, participating in a ministry that provides food to hungry families, or by helping children with schoolwork. Following Jesus' example of humble service was a major emphasis of the early church and has remained essential to Christian tradition ever since.

Our Eternal Companion

Much as your parents, pastors, teachers, and coaches will worry about whether they've adequately prepared you to leave their care, it is likely that you also will have some anxiety about leaving them behind as you move on to the next phase of life. And though you will probably maintain a connection with some or all these people, your relationship with them will change.

Jesus said quite a bit to his disciples on his final night with them about how their relationship would change. He would no longer be present with them in human form, but he had no plans of abandoning them. Jesus promised to send a "Companion"—or "Comforter" or "Advocate"—who would be with them forever. This Companion is God's Holy Spirit, who is with us at all times and in all places.

In the original Greek, Jesus in John's Gospel calls the Holy Spirit *Paraclete*, a Greek word that translates as "companion" or "advocate." *Paraclete* suggests the Spirit is on our side, looking out for us. However, other New Testament writers use the Greek word *Pneuma* to talk about the Holy Spirit. *Pneuma* means "wind" or "breath." We cannot see the Holy Spirit, just as we cannot see wind. But, as is the case with wind, we can feel the Spirit's presence and power.

Jesus tells us that this power or presence is with us always, guiding us and drawing us toward Christ. It is the Spirit who gives us the strength to put off buying the new pair of shoes we'd been wanting and instead donating the money we would have spent to a ministry that provides shoes to children in developing nations who don't have shoes. It is the Spirit who holds us back when we are tempted to spread a rumor that will embarrass one of our peers. And it is the Spirit who gives us the courage to press on in times of despair.

Jesus wanted his disciples to be aware of the Spirit and to embrace the Spirit. Jesus wants the same for us. Though relatively few people had the privilege of knowing God in the form of a human being who lived on earth, we all have the privilege of knowing God through the Holy Spirit.

Stay Connected

In the previous sessions you looked at Jesus' "I AM" statements. He made his final such statement during his final night with his disciples. "I am the vine; you are the branches," he said to them. "If you remain in me and I in you, then you will produce much fruit" (John 15:5). Even if you have only a rudimentary understanding of agriculture, you know that a branch of a tree or plant isn't going to blossom and produce fruit unless it's connected to a trunk, stem, or vine. A branch must connect to the part of the plant that is rooted in the ground in order to receive water and nutrients.

Jesus uses this botanical metaphor to describe our relationship with him. As branches we receive nourishment from Christ in the form of wisdom, courage, assurance, and grace. This nourishment enables us to be productive and fruitful servants of God.

As "branches," we must maintain a connection to Christ. We do this through spiritual habits such as daily prayer and weekly worship and by reading and studying Scripture. This connection to the "vine" allows us to bear fruit. The "fruit" in this metaphor are works of love, service, and obedience.

Jesus told his disciples, and still tells us today, that if we love him we will follow his commandments. While there are many commandments that Jesus would like us to obey, they all involve loving God and loving neighbor. Following his teaching about the vine and branches, Jesus said to his disciples, "This is my commandment: love each other just as I have loved you" (John 15:12).

If we are connected to Christ, the vine, we will bear fruit in the form of acts of love. As branches we should ask ourselves in every situation, "What is the most loving thing to do?" The answer will not always be clear, and there will be times when we answer this question incorrectly. But as we draw strength and nourishment from Christ and grow in faith, the way of love will become more apparent.

This idea, that love is at the heart of who we are as God's children and Christ's followers, isn't unique to the Gospel of John. We see it throughout Scripture. Jesus loved his disciples enough to wash their nasty feet. More importantly, Jesus loved all people enough to die for the forgiveness of our sins and to send the Holy Spirit to be present with us always. The Spirit gives us the strength to emulate Jesus by showing his incredible love to the people in our world today.

Session 4 Activities

Gathering Activity (Optional)

Get Logical

If you have not yet had time to finish it, continue working on the logic puzzle from Session 1. If you finish, check your answers with others in the group before looking at the answers at the end of the book. Remember that the inspiration for this activity comes from the opening chapter of John, which refers to Christ using the Greek word *Logos*, which is the root of the words *logic* and *logical*.

Large Group Activities

Wash Some Feet

All four Gospel writers tell us about Jesus' last night with his disciples, but John goes into much greater detail than his peers. Luke devotes 25 verses to this occasion, more than either Matthew or Mark. But John uses 155 verses—five full chapters. And it all starts with a foot washing. Discuss:

- What might cause someone's feet, in our time, to be especially dirty and disgusting?
- What sorts of feet would you most like to avoid? (For example, feet that have been walking around bare all day or feet that have just emerged after a two-hour soccer practice.)
- What are some undesirable jobs that you would rather do than wash someone else's dirty feet? Would you rather clean the cat's litter box? Would you rather scrub the toilet?

Read John 13:1-20.

There are plenty of ways for feet to get nasty in North America in the twenty-first century. But in the first-century Roman world, nasty feet were the norm.

Walking was the primary mode of transportation, and people wore only sandals or no shoes at all. Because feet got so dirty, household servants typically washed the feet of guests as a gesture of hospitality. On the evening before his death, Jesus took the role of a servant and washed his disciples' feet.

In remembrance of Jesus' act of humility and service, many churches do a foot-washing ceremony each year during Holy Week. You can hold a foot washing of your own. You'll need a basin of water and a washcloth and small towel for each participant.

Participants should sit in a circle and remove their shoes. One person will start with the basin. The person will dip the washcloth in the basin, use it to wash the feet of the person to the left, then dry that person's feet with a towel. Participants should not place washcloths back into the basin after washing feet. Continue around the circle until all have had a chance to wash someone's feet and have their feet washed.

Following the foot washing, discuss:

- Jesus told his disciples, "Just as I have done, you also must do." How can you follow Jesus' example by humbly serving others?

Advocate, Comforter, Companion

The books of the New Testament were written in *Koine* ("common") Greek. The original Greek words don't always have one clear English translation. Sometimes a single word or phrase can be translated in several ways. Such is the case with the word *Paraclete*, which Jesus uses in John 14 to describe the Holy Spirit. Depending on the version of the Bible you use, this word may be rendered as "Advocate," "Comforter," or "Companion."

Consider the word in context by reading John 14:25-26 and 15:26-27, preferably from different translations. Make note of what word these verses use to describe the Holy Spirit. Then look up each of the following words in an online dictionary:

- Advocate
- Comforter
- Companion

For each word, find the definition that you think best describes the Holy Spirit based on what Jesus says about the Spirit in the Gospel of John. Write these definitions on a markerboard or large sheet of paper. Then discuss:

- What is similar about these three definitions?
- What is unique about each definition?
- What does each definition tell you about who the Holy Spirit is and what the Holy Spirit does?

What Is He Talking About?

Jesus had a lot to say to his disciples on his final evening with them. Some of his words probably didn't make much sense to his disciples at the time. Divide into four teams. Each team will read one of the scriptures below, then summarize it for the rest of the group, focusing on these questions:

- What is Jesus teaching his disciples in this Scripture?
- What is Jesus teaching us?
- What questions might his disciples have had about this teaching?
- How might you answer these questions?
- What questions do you have?

All the scriptures should be used. Teams can have more than one.

- John 15:10-17
- John 15:18-21
- John 16:4-11
- John 16:17-24

Small Group Activities

Teams should be divided based on interest. There are activities for music, presentation, drama, and visual art.

Songs of the Spirit (music)

During his final evening with his disciples, Jesus assured them that, though he would be leaving them, the Holy Spirit would be present with them always. Of the three persons of the Trinity, the Holy Spirit is probably the one Christians talk about—and sing about—the least. God the Father and Jesus Christ function as characters in many popular Bible stories, making them relatable. We can talk about them and sing about them.

The Holy Spirit is more of an enigma. And it can be hard for us to think of and relate to the Spirit as a person. In the interest of getting to know the Spirit a little better, look through the hymnals or songbooks that your congregation uses and find two or three songs about the Holy Spirit. Prepare to teach the rest of your group. For each of the songs you find, discuss:

- What do the lyrics of this song or hymn tell us about who the Holy Spirit is?

If time permits, also discuss:

- If you were to write a praise song about the Holy Spirit, what would you want it to say about the Spirit?

Pass on Your Wisdom (presentation, older youth)

A team of older youth may work on creating a presentation for the benefit of the younger members of your group or the children in your congregation. Your goal is to impart wisdom and encouragement, as Jesus did with the disciples, and to give younger youth something to look forward to and aspire to. This presentation could take several forms:

- Create a slide show. If resources permit, put a presentation together using PowerPoint or another presentation software. (Some are available online for free.) You may include pictures of your experiences in the youth ministry along with words of advice and encouragement and relevant Bible verses.
- Make a poster. This poster could offer advice and encouragement to younger youth by featuring words of wisdom, appropriate Bible verses, and promos for opportunities available through your ministry.
- Give a talk. Pass along your wisdom the old-fashioned way, through the spoken word. Each member of your team should contribute something to the talk. Focus on being concise and helpful.

If you're having trouble coming up with ideas, organize your presentation using categories such as "Serving God," "Loving Neighbor," and "Growing in Faith."

You may not be able to complete your presentation in the time provided. But consider finishing it and including it in end-of-year activities.

What Else Happened at the Last Supper? (drama)

John's account of Jesus' final evening with his disciples is far more detailed than that of any other Gospel writers. In fact, nowhere else does the Bible devote so many verses to an event that lasts only a few hours. But despite all the information we have about that night, John's Gospel doesn't tell us everything.

Imagine something that went on during Jesus' last evening that isn't included in John's Gospel and present this moment in a skit. It may involve a side conversation among the disciples about something Jesus said or did; it may involve something that happened while they were preparing for dinner. As you put together your skit, consider that the disciples weren't fully aware of what would happen to Jesus in the coming days or of what would happen to them.

Consider the following questions as you work:

- What do you think Jesus' disciples were thinking and feeling as he washed their feet? as he said he would not be with them much longer?
- What questions do you think Jesus' disciples had (that they may or may not have asked)?
- What fears and worries do you think Jesus' disciples had? How might they have expressed those fears and worries?

Be prepared to present your skit to the rest of the group.

Prayer of St. Patrick (visual art)

Jesus taught that he is the vine and we are the branches. We need to remain connected to him so that we can receive spiritual nourishment and live fruitful, faithful lives. The Prayer of St. Patrick, part of which is below, is a famous Christian prayer about maintaining this connection to Christ. (The author of the prayer is actually anonymous and likely St. Patrick did not write it.)

Create a poster of this prayer. Write it in large letters and decorate the margins with appropriate pictures and symbols. You might draw inspiration from Jesus' teaching on the vine and branches from John 15:1-9.

The Prayer of St. Patrick

Christ with me, Christ before me, Christ behind me,
Christ in me, Christ beneath me, Christ above me,
Christ on my right, Christ on my left,
Christ when I lie down, Christ when I sit down,
Christ in the heart of everyone who thinks of me,
Christ in the mouth of everyone who speaks of me,
Christ in the eye that sees me,
Christ in the ear that hears me.

As you work, discuss what it means for Christ to be present with us, even though Christ no longer has a human body.

• • •

Teams should have plenty of time to complete their activities. Each group then can present what it did, created, or discussed. Following the presentations, discuss:

- What did you learn from these presentations about Jesus' final evening with his disciples?
- What else did you learn about how Christ is present with us and how God remains with us in the person of the Holy Spirit?

Closing

To close, each participant should complete each of these sentences:

- I feel God's Holy Spirit in my life when…
- I can connect with and grow closer to Christ by…

After everyone has had plenty of time to reflect on these sentences, go around the room, with each person completing both sentences verbally.

As time permits, read together John 17:1-26, Jesus' prayer for his disciples. Talk about how Jesus' prayer applies to us today. Then close in prayer.

God of Christ and the Holy Spirit, thank you for caring enough for us to live among us as Jesus and then to send your Spirit to live with us forever. Nourish us that we may grow in our relationships with you and bear the fruit of your love. We pray these things in Jesus' name. Amen.

5

THE ARREST, TRIAL, AND CRUCIFIXION OF THE KING

*Pilate said to the Jewish leaders, "Here's your king." The Jewish
leaders cried out, "Take him away! Take him away! Crucify him!"
Pilate responded, "What? Do you want me to crucify your king?"
"We have no king except the emperor," the chief priests answered.
Then Pilate handed Jesus over to be crucified.*

*The soldiers took Jesus prisoner. Carrying his cross by himself, he
went out to a place called Skull Place (in Aramaic,* Golgotha).
*That's where they crucified him—and two others with him, one
on each side and Jesus in the middle. Pilate had a public notice
written and posted on the cross. It read "Jesus the Nazarene, the
king of the Jews." Many of the Jews read this sign, for the place
where Jesus was crucified was near the city and it was written in
Aramaic, Latin, and Greek.*

(John 19:14b-20)

King is one of the many names and titles that Christians frequently use to
describe Jesus. This title has become so commonplace that we seldom stop to think
about what it means. We know that Jesus was a traveling teacher and healer and
that, while he certainly had followers and people who supported him financially,
he didn't have a realm, he didn't command an army, and he didn't have any of the
other resources we normally associate with kings. We also know he died a painful,
humiliating death.

Most of the people in Galilee and Judea during Jesus' time would have found the idea of Jesus as king to be absurd or even offensive. And, as far as they were concerned, any royal claim that Jesus did have would have ended when he was nailed to the cross. But for the author of John's Gospel, it was Jesus' suffering and death that made him king. By dying on the cross, he secured a victory greater than any an earthly king could boast.

Like a Boss

When have you had to do something important, even necessary, that you knew would be painful? Perhaps you have an aversion to going to the doctor but had to endure a medical examination in order to go on a mission trip or to play a sport. Maybe you had to hike several miles through rugged terrain in order to witness a natural wonder such as a waterfall or rock formation.

Jesus knew he had to endure a trial, suffering, and death to accomplish his purpose. Matthew, Mark, and Luke show Jesus in the garden before his arrest, agonizing about what he was about to face. "My Father," he said in Matthew 26:39, "if it's possible, take this cup of suffering away from me." But we don't see this in John's Gospel.

All the Gospels tell us that Jesus was arrested following his final meal with his disciples. John tells us that Judas—the disciple who betrayed Jesus—arrived with a "cohort" or "company" of troops to arrest Jesus. A company or cohort consisted of approximately six hundred soldiers. That's a lot of troops for the arrest of a man not known to be violent. But the soldiers were more intimidated by Jesus than he was by them.

When the troops said they were looking for Jesus the Nazarene and Jesus said to them, "I Am," the entire cohort shrank back and fell to the ground. You will recall from Session 3 that "I Am" was the ancient Hebrew name for God. By saying, "I Am," Jesus identified himself both as the person the troops were looking for and as God. No wonder the cohort fell over in shock. Jesus didn't take advantage of the fact that the arresting troops were on the ground, shrinking away from him. He knew what awaited him, and he faced it willingly and with confidence.

The Whole Truth and Nothing but the Truth

As you'd expect, a trial followed Jesus' arrest. In Matthew, Mark, and Luke, Jesus went on trial before the Sanhedrin, a large assembly of religious leaders. But in John he appeared first before Annas, the former high priest, then before Caiaphas, the current high priest. Both priests felt that Jesus' claims to be divine were dangerous and that Jesus should be executed. They sent him to Pilate, the local Roman governor.

Pilate wasn't Jewish and generally didn't get involved in religious matters. His priority was to keep the peace and establish Roman authority in Judea. Pilate didn't really care about Jesus claiming to be God. If Jesus claimed to be a king, however, Pilate had a problem. The Roman government didn't tolerate anyone who challenged its authority.

When Pilate asked Jesus if he claimed to be "king of the Jews," Jesus answered him with a question: "Do you say this on your own or have others spoken to you about me?" (John 18:34). This confused Pilate. Then Jesus said something that confused him even more: "My kingdom doesn't originate from this world" (18:36).

These strange answers may have frustrated Pilate, but they didn't convince him that Jesus deserved a death sentence. Pilate condemned Jesus to death not because Jesus was guilty but because Pilate wanted to keep the peace. (The historical record tells us that Pilate was known for using violence to remind the people of Judea who was in charge.) Having Jesus killed would pacify the crowd that demanded his execution and would shut down the idea that Jesus was some sort of god or king. But Jesus wasn't the sort of king that Pilate—or nearly anyone else at the time—had in mind.

A Lamb to the Slaughter

John tells us that Jesus was condemned to death at noon on the day of preparation for Passover. The other Gospels have a different timeline, placing Jesus' death on the morning of the first day of Passover. Passover is the Jewish festival commemorating the Israelites' deliverance from slavery in Egypt. The word itself refers to the final event in the Israelites' struggle for freedom: a plague that took the lives of the firstborn sons in every Egyptian family. Death "passed over" the Israelites' homes if they had followed God's instructions to slaughter a lamb and sprinkle its blood on their doorposts.

According to John, Jesus was the ultimate Passover lamb. Much as the lambs had been sacrificed for the lives and freedom of the ancient Israelites, Jesus sacrificed himself for the lives and freedom of all people. And, in John's Gospel, Jesus was killed on the day of preparation while the priests in the temple were ritually killing all the other Passover lambs.

Unlike Jesus, the ordinary sheep killed for Passover didn't have to suffer death on a cross. Crucifixion was a very painful and public form of execution. Criminals who died on crosses were displayed for everyone to see. The displays served as warnings to anyone who might threaten the peace of Rome. For this reason a sign attached to each cross explained what the criminal had done. Jesus' sign read, "Jesus the Nazarene, king of the Jews" translated into three languages: Aramaic, a language used by the Jewish people; Greek, the language of the eastern part of the Roman Empire where Jesus lived; and Latin, the language of Rome itself. For John, these translations signified that Jesus was king not only of the Jewish people, but of the entire world. And Jesus was revealed to be King in his death.

Saved From, Saved For

John goes out of his way to show that Jesus saved us from death and freed us from sin the same way that the Passover lamb saved the Israelites from death and freed them from slavery. But how does this work? How does a brutal execution two thousand years ago in another part of the world deliver us from sin and give us eternal life? The word we use to describe what Christ did for us on the cross is *atonement*, and Christians throughout history have understood atonement using three basic models:

- *Christus Victor* (**Christ the Victor**): This theory said that the powers of evil and death took hold of humanity when the first humans sinned in the garden of Eden. Death had claimed every person up to that point, but it couldn't claim Christ because Christ was without sin. Jesus defeated death, freeing sinful humanity from the clutches of evil. Versions of this model were widely accepted for the first millennium of Christianity.
- **Satisfaction Theory:** This model says that, by sinning against God, humanity owes a debt to God that sinful humans cannot possibly repay. But God, by becoming human in the person of Jesus, could pay the debt

on our behalf. By sacrificing himself, Jesus—who was without sin—paid the price for our sins. Anselm of Canterbury developed this model in the eleventh century, and it has been popular in the church ever since.

- **Moral Influence Theory:** According to this theory, in showing sacrificial love by dying on the cross, Jesus inspires us to make positive moral changes. Those who follow Christ reflect his unselfish love, transforming their hearts and the world as a result. This view has been most common in Eastern Christianity (the church in Eastern Europe, Asia, the Middle East, and parts of Africa). Some who hold this view also subscribe to one of the other models.

Regardless of how we understand atonement, followers of Jesus should reflect on two questions:

1. What does Christ save us from? Traditionally, we say that Jesus saved us from sin and death. But what does it mean for us to be free from sin, especially since we keep sinning? And what does it mean for us to be free from death, especially since we keep dying?
2. What does Christ save us for? While we should be thankful for all that Jesus has saved us from, accepting this gift of salvation is not the end of our faith story. Ephesians 2:10 tells us that we were created "to do good things. God planned for these good things to be the way that we live our lives." Jesus has shown extraordinary love to us so that we might show that love to others.

In John, Jesus' final words from the cross were "It is completed" (John 19:30). Some translations say, "It is finished." We might say, "It's over" or "I'm done." The meaning of the phrases varies depending on context and the attitude with which we say them. "It is finished" can mean, "I give up and can't go on" or "I did it!" It seems clear that in John, Jesus uttered the phrase in triumph. What do you think Jesus' last words meant?

Session 5 Activities

Gathering Activity (Optional)

Get Logical

If you have not yet had time to finish it, continue working on the logic puzzle from Session 1. If you finish, check your answers with others in the group before looking at the answers at the end of the book. Remember that the inspiration for this activity comes from the opening chapter of John, which refers to Christ using the Greek word *Logos*, which is the root of the words *logic* and *logical*.

Large Group Activities

Were You There When They Crucified My Lord?

As you gather, think of questions you have about the final hours of Jesus' life, including his arrest, trial, and execution. List these questions on a markerboard or large sheet of paper.

Go through the questions one by one. For which of the questions do members of your group think they have an answer? For which are they genuinely unsure? Which questions are people most curious about?

Keep these questions in mind as you go through the activities for this session. Note that this study focuses on the Gospel of John. Some of the questions you have might have answers in one of the other Gospels but not in John. And, for some of your questions, the different Gospel writers may have different answers or interpretations.

Compare and Contrast

Divide into five teams or pairs. Each team will read side-by-side accounts of Jesus' final days from one of the Synoptic Gospels and from the Gospel of John. One team will read the accounts of Jesus' arrest. Another will read the accounts of Jesus' trial before the religious leaders. The third will read the accounts of Jesus' trial before Pilate. The fourth will look at the crowd's response to Jesus' trial. And the fifth will read the accounts of Jesus' crucifixion. Each team will discuss the following:

- In what ways are the two accounts similar? How are they different?
- What seems to be most important to each Gospel writer?

Arrest
- Matthew 26:47-56
- John 18:1-14

Trial Before Religious Leaders
- Mark 14:53-65
- John 18:19-24

Trial Before Pilate
- Luke 23:1-12
- John 18:28-38; 19:8-16

The Crowd's Response
- Luke 23:13-25
- John 18:38–19:7

Jesus' Crucifixion
- Matthew 27:32-54
- John 19:16-37

Out of This World

Jesus tells Pilate, "My kingdom doesn't originate from this world" (John 18:36). Each of us is a citizen of a particular country and community. But as Jesus' followers our ultimate allegiance is to God's kingdom. As a group, brainstorm a list of rules we must follow and responsibilities we have as citizens of a nation and community. (Examples include paying taxes, registering vehicles, and properly disposing of trash.) Then brainstorm a second list of obligations and responsibilities we have as citizens of God's kingdom. (Examples include loving enemies, worshiping with a community of faith, and giving generously to those in need.)

Look over your two lists. Discuss:

- Which list of rules and responsibilities is most difficult to adhere to? Why?
- When might these two lists conflict with each other?
- How can we make loyalty to God's kingdom our top priority?

Small Group Activities

Divide into teams based on interest. There are activities for music, visual art, history, and drama.

Metaphor in Song (music)

Any good songwriter knows how to make effective use of a metaphor. In the Gospel of John, the timing of Jesus' trial and execution lends itself to a great metaphor: Jesus is the ultimate Passover lamb, slaughtered so that people may be delivered from death. This was an effective metaphor for the ancient Jewish people, but it doesn't work as well for twenty-first-century Americans with little knowledge of Judaism.

Work together as a team to identify a metaphor for Jesus' sacrifice that would resonate with a current-day audience. Then come up with a simple song that uses this metaphor to explain what Jesus did for us and what Jesus means for us. You might compose your song using four-line stanzas in this format:

Jesus is the [insert metaphor],

Because he _____ ,

And he _____ ,

And he _____ .

After agreeing on a metaphor and a tune, each person could come up with one stanza. Be prepared to teach your song to the rest of the group.

Stations of the Cross (visual art)

The stations of the cross is a Christian tradition involving a series of fourteen locations or images representing Jesus' suffering and execution. In many churches during Holy Week, worshipers go through the stations, stopping at each one to reflect on the image and pray.

Create stations-of-the-cross images for each of the following scenes (or for as many of the scenes as time permits), referring to the Scriptures for details and explanations:

1. Jesus in the garden (John 18:1-2; see also Matthew 26:36-46)
2. Jesus betrayed by Judas and arrested (John 18:3-14)
3. Jesus condemned by religious leaders (John 18:19-24)
4. Jesus denied by Peter (John 18:15-18, 25-27)
5. Jesus condemned by Pilate (John 18:28-40; 19:8-16)
6. Jesus crowned with a crown of thorns (John 19:1-6)
7. Jesus takes up his cross (Luke 23:26)
8. Simon the Cyrene helps Jesus carry his cross (Matthew 27:32)
9. Jesus meets the women of Jerusalem (Luke 23:27-31)
10. Jesus on the cross (John 19:18-24)
11. Jesus and the repentant thief (Luke 23:39-43)
12. Jesus entrusts his mother to the disciple he loved and vice versa (John 19:25-27)
13. Jesus dies (John 19:28-30)
14. Jesus in the tomb (John 19:38-42)

Be prepared to present your stations to the rest of the group. If possible, complete your stations in time for the next Holy Week.

The Gruesome Details (history)

For centuries, Christians have identified themselves with the symbol of the cross. It's a reminder of the death that Jesus suffered to win our salvation. But what do you actually know about crucifixion? Do some research on the practice, considering the following questions:

- What was the purpose of crucifixion? Why were certain people sentenced to death on a cross instead of by another form of execution?
- How did crucifixion work? What was the cause of death?
- In what cultures was crucifixion a common practice?
- Is crucifixion still practiced today? If so, where?

Based on your findings, why do you think Jesus was crucified? Does your new knowledge affect how you think of the sacrifice that Jesus made on our behalf?

Jesus on Trial (drama)

Imagine that you are the Roman governor in Judea, and some religious leaders bring a man before you to be executed. The people insist that the man should die for his crimes but aren't entirely clear about what his crimes are. You get the impression that the man has somehow disrespected their god or their beliefs, and you've heard that he considers himself some sort of king.

Create a skit in which you ask questions of this man and of his accusers. What would you ask to get a better idea of why the religious leaders want you to execute the man? What would you ask the man to determine whether he is guilty of what he's been accused of? After all the questioning, what verdict would you render, and how would you justify it?

As you create your skit, reflect on what the people involved in Jesus' trial—Pilate, his accusers, the people yelling for his execution, those who sympathized with him—would have been thinking and feeling.

• • •

Teams should have plenty of time to complete their activities. Then each group can present what it did, created, or discussed. Following the presentations, discuss:

- What did you learn from these presentations about Jesus' arrest, trial, and crucifixion?

Closing

To close, revisit the questions you came up with as part of the opening activity. Go through the questions one by one. For which questions do you have answers (if only partial ones)? Which questions remain unanswered? What new questions do you have?

Go around the room and name one thing everyone has learned about Jesus' suffering and death. Then close in prayer.

God of sacrifice and atonement, thank you for becoming human, suffering, and dying to deliver us from sin and death. Give us the strength to follow your example by facing our trials with courage and faith and by giving of ourselves for others. In the name of Christ, who faced and defeated death, we pray. Amen.

6

ETERNAL LIFE

There was a garden in the place where Jesus was crucified, and in the garden was a new tomb in which no one had ever been laid. Because it was the Jewish Preparation Day and the tomb was nearby, they laid Jesus in it.... Early in the morning of the first day of the week, while it was still dark, Mary Magdalene came to the tomb and saw that the stone had been taken away from the tomb.... Mary stood outside near the tomb, crying. As she cried, she bent down to look into the tomb. She saw two angels dressed in white, seated where the body of Jesus had been, one at the head and one at the foot. The angels asked her, "Woman, why are you crying?" She replied, "They have taken away my Lord, and I don't know where they've put him." As soon as she had said this, she turned around and saw Jesus standing there, but she didn't know it was Jesus. Jesus said to her, "Woman, why are you crying? Who are you looking for?" Thinking he was the gardener, she replied, "Sir, if you have carried him away, tell me where you have put him and I will get him." Jesus said to her, "Mary." She turned and said to him in Aramaic, "Rabbouni" (which means Teacher).... Mary Magdalene left and announced to the disciples, "I've seen the Lord." Then she told them what he said to her.

(John 19:41-42, 20:1, 11-16, 18)

Imagine being one of Jesus' disciples on the day of his execution. You had devoted three years of your life (according to John's version of events) to following a man you believed to be the Messiah. You had left your family, home, and livelihood because you believed that Jesus would bring about a new reality for God's people.

Then he was sentenced to die. On a cross. Where he would suffer and where anyone could watch him die. And, since crucifixion was usually reserved for people the government viewed as a threat, there was a pretty good chance that Pilate and company would be looking to round up Jesus' close followers and kill them too.

What would you do in their situation? How would you go on?

The good news for the disciples is that they only had to spend a couple days in agony before getting the word that Jesus was alive. His story didn't end on the cross. Because of Jesus, our story doesn't end with death, either.

Sadness and Fear

All the Gospel writers agree that Mary Magdalene was the first person to visit Jesus' tomb and find it empty. Mary was one of Jesus' closest followers. Luke tells us that Jesus had healed Mary of "seven demons," meaning that she likely had a troubled past, and that Mary supported Jesus financially (Luke 8:3). The fact that she is called "Magdalene," meaning "from Magdala," means that she was probably single. Married women at the time often were referred to using their husbands' names ("Mary, wife of _____"). Contrary to popular belief, the Bible never says that Mary was a prostitute.

John tells us that Mary stood at the foot of the cross when Jesus was crucified, and on the morning of the Sunday following Jesus' death—the first Easter morning—she was the first person to visit the tomb. When she arrived, she found that the large stone sealing the entrance to the tomb had been removed and that the tomb itself was empty. Nowadays we think of the empty tomb as a cause for celebration, but in that moment Mary probably wasn't thinking that Jesus had risen. Her first thought was that someone had moved the body or even stolen it.

Alarmed, Mary ran to tell Peter and the disciple "whom Jesus loved" (traditionally identified as John) about what she had seen. The two disciples returned with her to the tomb, but they didn't stick around. Mary did. And while she was there, crying, Jesus appeared before her, but she didn't recognize him. She assumed he was the gardener. It wasn't until Jesus spoke her name that she realized who he was. We don't know what was going through Mary's mind in that moment. Did she understand that Jesus had returned to life in a new, perfect, eternal body? Did she think she was hallucinating or seeing a ghost? Regardless of what she was thinking, she hurried to tell the disciples what she had experienced.

While Mary responded to Jesus' death with sadness, Jesus' disciples responded with fear. They had seen the religious and political authorities arrest and execute their leader even though Jesus had done nothing to warrant a trial or punishment. They had every reason to assume they would be next. So they went into hiding. They didn't meet Jesus outside the tomb. Instead they met him where they were gathered behind closed and locked doors. (Locked doors kept the disciples safe from those who might be looking to kill or arrest them but were no obstacle for Jesus.)

The sadness we see in Mary and the fear we see in the disciples are possibly the two most common human responses to death. The finality of death—the end of our lives on earth and the end of our relationships with loved ones—causes sorrow and anxiety. Both are reasonable responses. But because of what happened on that first Easter morning, we know that death does not have the final say and that we can also approach death with hope, courage, and joy.

Don't Just Talk About It; Live It

Throughout his ministry, Jesus had spoken of resurrection and eternal life. In the Gospel of John's most famous verse Jesus says, "God so loved the world that he gave his only Son, so that everyone who believes in him won't perish but will have eternal life" (John 3:16). When his friend Lazarus died, Jesus had promised Lazarus's sister, Martha, that her brother would rise again. Jesus then referred to himself as "the resurrection and the life." He said, "Whoever believes in me will live, even though they die" (John 11:25). And on the night before his death, Jesus told his disciples that he was going to his Father's house to prepare a room for them.

Eternal life and the resurrection of the dead were ideas that existed among Jewish people in the first century. Such ideas would have resonated with people who were poor, oppressed, and powerless. But they were just ideas. No one had witnessed the resurrection of the dead. No one had seen a human being overcome death and take on a perfect, immortal body. Until Jesus. Jesus' resurrection turned words and ideas into reality.

As Jesus' followers we live in a new reality, one where death isn't the end of life but is just another step along the way. That doesn't mean we should just sit back and wait to be resurrected. When Jesus met up with his disciples after his resurrection he told them, "As my Father sent me, so I am sending you" (John 20:21). Later, when Jesus met with Peter on the shore of the Sea of Galilee, he asked Peter three times, "Do you love me?" Each time, when Peter answered yes, Jesus instructed Peter to feed his sheep. Jesus had called himself the "good shepherd." His "sheep" were God's people, including those who had not yet found their way to the flock.

We are people of the Resurrection, living in a world full of death and despair. We have a responsibility to bring the hope of Christ to those who are suffering from fear, sadness, hunger, disease, abuse, addiction, bullying, and countless other examples of pain and brokenness. We offer them hope, not just through words and ideas but through our actions, our presence, our time, our patience, and our forgiveness.

Jesus promised us eternal life. And he delivered on that promise. Toward the end of John's Gospel, the author explains his purpose for writing the book. "These things are written so that you will believe that Jesus is the Christ, God's Son, and that believing, you will have life in his name" (John 20:31). Those of us who have heard the story and now believe can live as people of courage, hope, and joy, knowing that death cannot defeat us. Like John, we can tell the story so that those who hear it and experience it may know the courage, hope, and joy that we have known.

Session 6 Activities

Gathering Activity (Optional)

Get Logical

If you have not yet had time to finish it, continue working on the logic puzzle from Session 1. If you finish, check your answers with others in the group before looking at the answers at the end of the book. Remember that the inspiration for this activity comes from the opening chapter of John, which refers to Christ using the Greek word *Logos*, which is the root of the words *logic* and *logical*.

Large Group Activities

Happy Easter

As you gather, brainstorm a list of some of your favorite Easter traditions. Once most people are present and you have a pretty good list, go through each of the items and talk about why it might be part of our Easter celebrations. While Easter often becomes a festival of eggs, rabbits, and candy, it is meant to be the day when we celebrate Jesus' resurrection and victory over death. Why might some of these other traditions have developed? What do eggs and rabbits have to do with resurrection and eternal life? Discuss:

- What do you know about the story of Easter?
- What questions do you have about Jesus' resurrection?

List any questions you have on a markerboard or large sheet of paper so that you can refer back to them during your time together.

Words of Resurrection

On many occasions during his ministry, Jesus had mentioned his resurrection and the promise of life after death. When Jesus rose from the dead and appeared before his followers on Easter morning, these words took on new and greater meaning.

Divide into three teams. Each team should read one of the following scriptures and discuss the questions below as they pertain to the assigned scripture.

- John 3:14-17 (Refer to Numbers 21:4-9 for more information about Moses lifting up the snake in the wilderness.)
- John 11:17-44
- John 14:1-6

Questions:

- What does Jesus say about resurrection or eternal life in this scripture?
- What about Jesus' teaching may have been confusing to those who heard it? What might they have misunderstood?

After each team has had about five minutes to read and discuss its scripture, each team can summarize its verses and answers to the questions.

Feed My Sheep

Read aloud John 18:15-18, 25-27 in which Peter denied Jesus three times while Jesus was on trial. This was a bad moment for Peter, but it wasn't the end of his story.

Read aloud John 21:15-18 in which Jesus, after his resurrection, appeared to his disciples while they were fishing on the Sea of Galilee, then cooked them breakfast and had a moment with Peter. Discuss:

- How many times did Jesus ask Peter, "Do you love me?" What might be the significance of this number?
- What do you think Jesus meant when he told Peter, "Feed my lambs" or "Take care of my sheep" or "Feed my sheep"? Who are Jesus' sheep?
- What does this scripture say about the connection between loving Jesus and loving other people?
- What are some ways that our congregation and youth ministry feed Jesus' sheep?
- What are some ways that you, as an individual, could feed Jesus' sheep?

Small Group Activities

Divide into teams based on interest. There are activities for visual art, drama, music, and illusion.

Jesus, I Didn't Recognize You (visual art)

Read John 20:11-18. While Mary was standing at Jesus' tomb crying, she found herself in a conversation with a man she assumed was a gardener. But when the man said her name, she realized she was talking to Jesus, resurrected from death. Luke 24:13-35 contains a similar story. Two disciples chat with the risen Jesus over the course of a seven-mile walk but don't recognize who he is until they arrive at their destination and he breaks bread with them.

These scriptures suggest that there was something different about Jesus' resurrected body that kept even his closest friends and followers from recognizing him at first. But at times, all of us have failed to recognize Jesus when we have encountered him. In Matthew 25:31-40, Jesus tells us that whenever we serve those who are vulnerable or in need, we serve him. We also know that Jesus speaks to us through people in our lives and through situations. Like Mary, we just don't always recognize him at first.

Individually, create pictures of the Jesus you didn't recognize. You could illustrate a time when you encountered someone who was stranded or lonely or hungry; Jesus was present in this person, even if you didn't realize it at the time. You could illustrate a situation where you felt an overwhelming sense of peace or confidence; perhaps you later understood that Jesus was with you in that moment. You could create a portrait of a friend or family member in whom you see the love of Christ.

Be prepared to present your drawings and talk about the Jesus we don't recognize.

Forever a Doubter (drama)

What do you know about Jesus' disciple Thomas? Have you ever heard someone called a "doubting Thomas"? The moment most associated with Thomas comes from John 20:24-29. Jesus had appeared to his disciples in his resurrected body, but Thomas had not been with them. When the other disciples told Thomas what they had seen, he was reluctant to believe them. Fortunately, Jesus appeared to Thomas personally to put an end to his doubts.

But speaking about Thomas as a doubter may be unfair. Read John 11:1-16. Discuss how this scripture changes your view of Thomas. Then work together to create a skit in which a group of Jesus' followers joke with Thomas about being a doubter and in which Thomas gives his side of the story. The other disciples and followers might include Peter, James, John, Mary, and Martha.

Be prepared to present your skit and lead a discussion of these questions:

- What might cause someone to doubt the story of Christ?
- When have you worked through doubts about your faith?
- Do you think Thomas was right to be doubtful? Why or why not?

Walking Through Walls (illusion)

Read John 20:19-31. Following his resurrection, Jesus twice appeared to his disciples when they were meeting behind closed doors. John tells us that in one case the doors were even locked. In his resurrected body, Jesus could apparently walk through walls. In remembrance of the risen Christ's ability to move through solid matter, learn an illusion in which you'll make a quarter appear to pass through a solid table.

Start by placing a quarter on the table. Rest your left hand in your lap. Put your right hand on the coin and slide it back along the table. You want to give the impression that you are picking up the coin in your right hand by palming it. In actuality, you want the coin to fall off the table and into your left hand. It is essential that the "audience" doesn't see the coin fall.

Smack your right hand down on the table. If you've been discreet enough in your movements, your audience will assume that the quarter has been in your hand the entire time. Pull your left hand from beneath the table to reveal the quarter. It should appear as though the quarter passed through the table.

As a team, take turns practicing this trick, and be prepared to show it to the larger group. After you've practiced the trick, discuss:

- What might the disciples have been thinking when Jesus appeared before them while they were behind closed doors?
- What does this scripture tell us about Jesus' resurrected body and how it was changed?

● ● ●

Teams should have plenty of time to complete their activities. Then each group can present what it did, created, or discussed. Following the presentations, discuss:

- What did you learn from these presentations about Jesus' resurrection and what it means for us, his followers?

Closing

To close, revisit the questions you listed as part of the opening activity. Go through the questions. For which questions do you have answers? Which questions remain unanswered? What new questions do you have?

Then take two minutes in silence to reflect on what you've learned and discussed over the past several weeks. When two minutes have passed, go around the room and each person should name one thing to remember from this study. It may be something learned about the Gospel of John, something mentioned in a discussion that was particularly meaningful, or something experienced during an activity. Then close in prayer.

God of resurrection, you promised us eternal life, and you followed up on that promise. Give us the courage to live as people of the Resurrection. Thank you for becoming human and suffering and dying to deliver us from sin and death. Give us the strength to follow your example by facing our trials with courage and faith and by giving of ourselves for others. As your followers, we know that we will experience hardship but because of the hardship you endured, we can look forward to something greater. In the name of Christ, who faced and defeated death, we pray. Amen.

Answers to Gathering Activity puzzle, "Get Logical":

- James came from Corinth and brought wine.
- John came from Alexandria and brought bread.
- Martha came from Ephesus and brought figs
- Mary came from Rome and brought olive oil.
- Peter came from Antioch and brought fish.